G. ALLEN

M000035949

THE

MOST

ABUNDANT

LIFE

FEARLESS LIVING IN FRIGHTENING TIMES

Copyright © 2015 by G. Allen Jackson for "The Most Abundant Life, Fearless Living in Frightening Times".

Published by Intend® Publishing
1921 New Salem Road, Hwy. 99
Murfreesboro, TN 37128

Special Sales:
Most Intend® books are available at special quantity discounts when purchased in bulk by corporations, organizations, and special-interest groups. Custom imprinting or excerpting can also be done to fit special needs. For more information, please email contact@intendministries.org.

Unless otherwise noted, all Scripture quotes are taken from the HOLY BIBLE, NEW INTERNATIONAL VERSION®. Copyright © 1973, 1978, and 1984 by International Bible Society. Used by permission of Zondervan Bible Publishing House. All rights reserved.

The "NIV" and "New International Version" trademarks are registered in the United States Patent and Trademark Office by Biblica. Use of either trademark requires the permission of Biblica.

All rights reserved. No part of this publication may be reproduced in any form, except for brief quotations in reviews, without the written permission of the author.

Contents

G. Allen Jackson

Senior Pastor, World Outreach Church

Is there a God who cares about me? Can I know His plan and purpose for my life? Is it presumptuous to ask God for something? Questions such as these bubble up in all of our thoughts. We want to believe we are not alone. We are aware enough of our limits to be interested in help. Often our religious experiences have suggested we should not "bother God" with trivial things. Fortunately, we have the Bible. God has provided us with His perspective. For the next few weeks we are going to explore what God has to say about our quality of life. The good news is we are not left to wonder; Almighty God has clearly communicated His intent toward us.

We live in a turbulent world. Evil exists. Life under the sun is challenging. Often it seems our dreams are under a full-scale assault by forces beyond our control. Yet the light of God always overcomes the darkness. We are designed to thrive in the light, to move toward the light. God's truth within our hearts enables us to live fearlessly, even in frightening times.
God cares for His people!

The revelation of God's will begins in the first verses of our Bible. Adam and Eve were given a garden of amazing abundance. Our first insight into God's character and interest in humanity is revealed in those first verses of the Bible. When God imagined the earth, He designed it with complete provision; then He gave authority over all His creation to Adam and his descendants. This notion of God's abundant provision for His people is consistent throughout the story of Scripture. When God delivered the Hebrew slaves, He led them into the wilderness where He provided abundantly for their needs. Jesus reminded us that if we would seek first the Kingdom of God, all of our needs would be abundantly addressed.

In spite of the clear invitation of Scripture, we struggle to trust the Lord. We wrestle inwardly with the whispers of doubt: Can Almighty God, the creator of heaven and earth, really be trusted with my well-being? As you walk through the weeks of this study, open your heart to the Holy Spirit. Listen to the questions and experiences of the others joining you in the journey. Embrace God's Word as a personal promise. God is still watching over His people in the earth. He is well able to lead us into the most abundant life.

Fearless Living in Frightening Times

Outline
For Each Session

A typical group session for The Most Abundant Life study will include the following:

GETTING STARTED. The foundation for spiritual growth is an intimate connection with God and His family. A few people who really know you and who earn your trust provide a place to experience the life Jesus invites you to live. Each session offers two options that will help your group get acquainted. Using the icebreaker enables the group to connect with one another and begin the discussion with ease.

DVD TEACHING SEGMENT. Serving as a companion to *The Most Abundant Life* study guide is the DVD video teaching. This DVD has helpful teaching segments from Pastor Allen Jackson.

DISCUSSION. This section is where you will process, as a group, the teaching you heard and saw. The focus will be on how we should live in light of the Word of God. We want to help you apply the insights from Scripture practically, creatively, and to your heart as well as your head. At the end of the day, allowing the timeless truths from God's Word to transform our lives in Christ is our greatest aim.

APPLICATION. The objective of studying the Bible is not primarily information; it is transformation. Each week we will walk through questions intended to help us not only learn but also put into practice biblical truth, which brings freedom.

DAILY DEVOTIONALS. Each week on the Daily Devotionals pages we provide Scriptures to read and reflect on between group meetings. We suggest you use this section to seek God on your own throughout the week. This time at home should begin and end with prayer. Don't get in a hurry; take enough time to hear God's direction.

WEEKLY MEMORY VERSES. For each session we have provided a Memory Verse that emphasizes an important truth from the session. This is an optional exercise, but we believe that memorizing Scripture can be a vital part of filling our minds with God's will for our lives. We encourage you to give this important habit a try.

ADDITIONAL STUDY. Each lesson is self-contained; however, for the persons who would like to prepare for the upcoming lesson, this section has tools available specifically for preparing in advance.

01

God Is the Source

A most abundant life is anchored in the character of God. Left to ourselves life is a struggle, for we are finite creatures. A vision of God and His interest in our well-being opens the windows of heavenly possibility. It is not presumption to trust in God; it is an expression of faith. God responds to the faith of His people. Doubt is a catalyst for despair. As you begin this study, ask God to let faith grow within you. Purposefully set aside your skepticism and doubt. A wonderful revelation of God's Word and His intent for you is just ahead.

getting

→ Begin your time together by using one or both of the following icebreakers.

Name a routine/habit you wish was part of your life.

What was your first job?

Outline of DVD Lesson

Use the outline below to follow along during the DVD. The answers to the blanks below can be found in the video.

GENESIS 8:22

"As long as the earth endures, seedtime and harvest, cold and heat, summer and winter, day and night will never cease."

ROMANS 5:17

For if, by the trespass of the one man, death reigned through that one man, how much more will those who receive God's abundant provision of grace and of the gift of righteousness reign in life through the one man, Jesus Christ!

God's ___abundant___ provision of grace enables us to lead triumphant lives.

God as Creator/Designer

PSALM 100:3 (NASB)

Know that the LORD Himself is God; it is He who has made us, and not we ourselves; we are His people, and the sheep of His pasture.

God made ___us___!

God of Abundance

1. In Diversity

GENESIS 1:20-21

[20] *And God said, "Let the water teem with living creatures, and let birds fly above the earth across the expanse of the sky."* [21] *So God created the great creatures of the sea and every living and moving thing with which the water teems, according to their kinds, and every winged bird according to its kind. And God saw that it was good.*

God is not _Stingy_ with us.

2. In Complexity

- We have ___60,000___ miles of blood vessels—enough to stretch almost 2.5 times around the earth.
  - A greater surface area than 3 tennis courts
  - For every additional pound of fat, our body produces 7 miles of blood vessels

- Our heart will pump nearly 1.5 million barrels of blood during our lifetime—enough to fill ___200___ train tank cars.

- If uncoiled, the DNA in our bodies would stretch 10 billion miles—that's from here to Pluto and back.

3. In Generosity

GENESIS 1:26
Then God said, "Let us make man in our image, in our likeness, and let them rule over the fish of the sea and the birds of the air, over the livestock, over all the earth, and over all the creatures that move along the ground."

He is the _Source_ of our lives.

Answers: abundant; us; stingy; 60,000; 200; Source

For we are God's handiwork, created in Christ Jesus to do good works, which God prepared in advance for us to do.

Ephesians 2:10

Discussion

Using the questions that follow, we will review and expand on the teaching we just experienced.

READ ALOUD

A sanctified life is a life set apart for God's purposes. To be "set apart" is to be unique. God's people are intended to be unique because we live with a courage fueled by faith. The knowledge of God will enable you to live fearlessly even in frightening times. Our future is secured by God's strength and resources—not our own.

GENESIS 8:22

"As long as the earth endures, seedtime and harvest, cold and heat, summer and winter, day and night will never cease."

1   In Genesis 8, God promises that some things will never cease. What are they?

2   List some of the steps in moving from seedtime to harvest.

READ ALOUD

Of the four pairs listed—seedtime and harvest, cold and heat, summer and winter, day and night—only one is dependent upon our activity. We cannot hasten the night or shorten the winter. However, we will forfeit the harvest if we ignore the seedtime or opportunity to plant. Often we want a harvest without the effort of seedtime.

ROMANS 5:17

For if, by the trespass of the one man, death reigned through that one man, how much more will those who receive God's abundant provision of grace and of the gift of righteousness reign in life through the one man, Jesus Christ!

3 Romans 5:17 describes God's intent for our lives. How are we to live?

4 We can reign in life because God has abundantly provided two things. What are they?

5 God has provided two things that are otherwise completely unattainable. Why do we have trouble trusting Him for all other things?

READ ALOUD

We owe everything to Jesus. His life and choices have provided an entirely new future for us. God's provision for our lives is based upon what Jesus did, not upon who or what we are.

PSALM 100:3 (NASB)

Know that the LORD Himself is God; it is He who has made us, and not we ourselves; we are His people and the sheep of His pasture.

6 Psalm 100 reminds us of our origin. How does it describe our relationship to God?

7 Is the revelation of God as Creator a struggle for you to accept? Why or why not?

Application

Now it is time to make some personal applications of all we have been thinking about in the last few minutes.

READ ALOUD

God's abundant provision is evident in creation in three distinct ways: diversity, complexity, and generosity. More than 100 species of roses exist, with thousands of variants resulting from cross breeding. The human eye can distinguish ten million different colors. If you will accept God as Creator, the entire discussion of faith is transformed.

8   What does the variety of flowers, birds, or fish suggest to you about the character of God?

MATTHEW 6:28-30

28 *"And why do you worry about clothes? See how the lilies of the field grow. They do not labor or spin.* 29 *Yet I tell you that not even Solomon in all his splendor was dressed like one of these.* 30 *If that is how God clothes the grass of the field, which is here today and tomorrow is thrown into the fire, will he not much more clothe you, O you of little faith?"*

9   Jesus told us God is concerned even with our clothing. Where are you tempted to doubt God's provision?

10   All of creation is a reminder of God's provision. It is for our benefit. Have you ever been reluctant to ask God for something? Why?

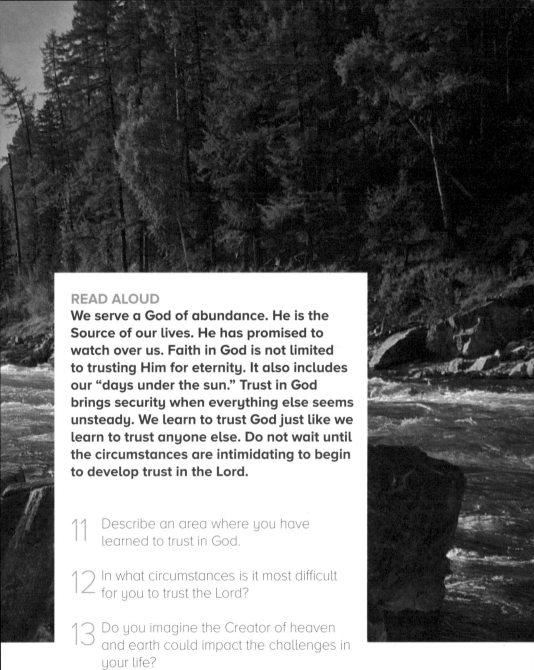

READ ALOUD

We serve a God of abundance. He is the Source of our lives. He has promised to watch over us. Faith in God is not limited to trusting Him for eternity. It also includes our "days under the sun." Trust in God brings security when everything else seems unsteady. We learn to trust God just like we learn to trust anyone else. Do not wait until the circumstances are intimidating to begin to develop trust in the Lord.

11 Describe an area where you have learned to trust in God.

12 In what circumstances is it most difficult for you to trust the Lord?

13 Do you imagine the Creator of heaven and earth could impact the challenges in your life?

14 Complete the sentence, "God is my source, I will not fear . . ."

Prayer

Close the session by reading this prayer together. Make it your prayer each day in the coming week.

Almighty God, Creator of heaven and earth, thank You for loving me. Your great mercy and compassion have brought hope to my life. Holy Spirit, help me to learn to trust more completely. I lay aside doubt, fear, and skepticism. I boldly proclaim that the promises of God are true for my life and my family. I believe God is able. Through the blood of Jesus Christ I am redeemed from an empty way of life and made a participant in the eternal Kingdom of my Lord. In His name I pray, amen.

PRAYER REQUEST

....
....
....
....
....
....
....
....
....

Additional Study

Each week's lesson is built to be self-contained. However, some like to prepare in advance for the next session. If this is you, visit us online for Pastor Allen's full sermon on each session as well as other tools for additional study in preparation for next week.

To prepare for next week, watch

Living Unafraid

TheMostAbundantLife.com

Daily Devotions

Day 1
Our Creator

Know that the Lord is God. It is he who made us, and we are his; we are his people, the sheep of his pasture.

PSALM 100:3

Day 2
God's Handiwork

For we are God's handiwork, created in Christ Jesus to do good works, which God prepared in advance for us to do.

EPHESIANS 2:10

Day 3
His Faithfulness

The heavens praise your wonders, Lord, your faithfulness too, in the assembly of the holy ones.

PSALM 89:5

reflection question:

Reflect on the unique characteristics He gave you.

reflection question:

What "good works" are you created for?

reflection question:

Take a moment and thank God for His faithfulness.

Memory Verse

Ephesians 2:10 — *For we are God's handiwork, created in Christ Jesus to do good works, which God prepared in advance for us to do.*

Day 4
Complex Creator

So God created the great creatures of the sea and every living thing...And God saw that it was good.

GENESIS 1:21

Day 5
Generous God

Then God said, "Let us make mankind in our image, in our likeness, so that they may rule over the fish in the sea and the birds in the sky, over the livestock and all the wild animals, and over all the creatures that move along the ground."

GENESIS 1:26

---

reflection question:

List one creature. Now, think about the variety and complexity wrapped up in that one creature.

reflection question:

Why do you suppose God did not withhold giving us rule over any living thing?

Study Notes

02

Living Unafraid

We have begun a journey learning about God's abundant provision for our lives. God is not an extraneous addition to our lives. A relationship with Jesus is foundational to contentment and joy. In this session, we will begin to consider God's provision as a stabilizing force on our behalf. Trust defeats fear. As we learn to trust God more fully, we can face life and all challenges fearlessly.

getting

 Begin your time together by using one or both of the following icebreakers.

Share something that makes you afraid (snakes, dark, etc.).

Do you sleep with a light on? Why or why not?

started

Outline of DVD Lesson

Use the outline below to follow along during the DVD. The answers to the blanks below can be found in the video.

GENESIS 8:22

"As long as the earth endures, seedtime and harvest, cold and heat, summer and winter, day and night will never cease."

GALATIANS 6:9

Let us not become weary in doing good, for at the proper time we will reap a harvest if we do not give up.

𝒲e will not _____!

Our Lives—Physical & Spiritual

A. In this world but not "of this _____"

HEBREWS 11:24-27

24 By faith Moses, when he had grown up, refused to be known as the son of Pharaoh's daughter. 25 He chose to be mistreated along with the people of God rather than to enjoy the pleasures of sin for a short time. 26 He regarded disgrace for the sake of Christ as of greater value than the treasures of Egypt, because he was looking ahead to his reward. 27 By faith he left Egypt, not fearing the king's anger; he persevered because he saw him who is invisible.

We live in tension between _____ *&*
eternity.

B. God Is Our Source

1. Physical Abundance

DEUTERONOMY 11:14-15
[14] *then I will send rain on your land in its season, both autumn and spring rains, so that you may gather in your grain, new wine and oil.*
[15] *I will provide grass in the fields for your cattle, and you will eat and be satisfied.*

God says He will _____ *us.*

2. Spiritual Abundance

2 CORINTHIANS 1:20
For no matter how many promises God has made, they are "Yes" in Christ. And so through him the "Amen" is spoken by us to the glory of God.

God says His _____ *will fill your lives.*

C. Why It Matters

1. Seasons of Less

PHILIPPIANS 4:12-13

[12] I know what it is to be in need, and I know what it is to have plenty. I have learned the secret of being content in any and every situation, whether well fed or hungry, whether living in plenty or in want.. [13] I can do everything through him who gives me strength.

2. Seasons of Uncertainty/Shaking

HEBREWS 12:26-29

[26] . . . but now he has promised, "Once more I will shake not only the earth but also the heavens." [27] The words "once more" indicate the removing of what can be shaken--that is, created things--so that what cannot be shaken may remain. [28] Therefore, since we are receiving a kingdom that cannot be shaken, let us be thankful, and so worship God acceptably with reverence and awe, [29] for our God is a consuming fire."

3. Do Not Be Deceived

MARK 4:18-19

[18] Still others, like seed sown among thorns, hear the word; [19] but the worries of this life, the deceitfulness of wealth and the desires for other things come in and choke the word, making it unfruitful.

Answers: quit; world; time; help; abundance

His divine power has given us everything we need for a godly life through our knowledge of him who called us by his own glory and goodness.

2 Peter 1:3

Discussion

Using the questions that follow, we will review and expand on the DVD presentation.

READ ALOUD
As Americans it is printed on our money, "In God We Trust." What a remarkable proclamation. As individuals we learn to trust in God. We grow in trust. This study is designed to help us learn to trust in ways we did not even know we had permission to do. The Bible says we perish "for lack of knowledge." During these weeks, ask God for an open heart to receive a revelation of His abundance for you.

GALATIANS 6:9
Let us not become weary in doing good, for at the proper time we will reap a harvest if we do not give up.

1   Do you ever become weary in doing wrong?

2   What is the condition required for a harvest?

3   Describe a time when you gave up "too soon."

HEBREWS 11:24-27
24 By faith Moses, when he had grown up, refused to be known as the son of Pharaoh's daughter. 25 He chose to be mistreated along with the people of God rather than to enjoy the pleasures of sin for a short time. 26 He regarded disgrace for the sake of Christ as of greater value than the treasures of Egypt, because he was looking ahead to his reward. 27 By faith he left Egypt, not fearing the king's anger; he persevered because he saw him who is invisible.

4   What did Moses refuse?

5   What did Moses choose?

6   What enabled Moses to persevere?

7   Moses was in a personal struggle between what he could see and what he could not. What could he see that suggested success was improbable? What could he see that suggested success was likely?

Application

Now it is time to make some personal applications of all we have been thinking about in the last few minutes.

READ ALOUD

We are complex beings. Life is not physical, mental, emotional, or spiritual. It is all of the above. It is helpful to grow in all arenas. Any part of our self that is ignored leaves us vulnerable. The Bible helps us understand that the spiritual world gave rise to our physical world. Understanding spiritual forces will change our lives physically, mentally, and emotionally. To ignore spiritual truth leaves us diminished physically, mentally, and emotionally.

8   Complete this sentence: I am a spirit; I live in a body; and I have a _____.

DEUTERONOMY 11:14-15

14 . . . then I will send rain on your land in its season, both autumn and spring rains, so that you may gather in your grain, new wine and oil. 15 I will provide grass in the fields for your cattle, and you will eat and be satisfied.

9   God is our Source. What does God promise to "send and provide"?

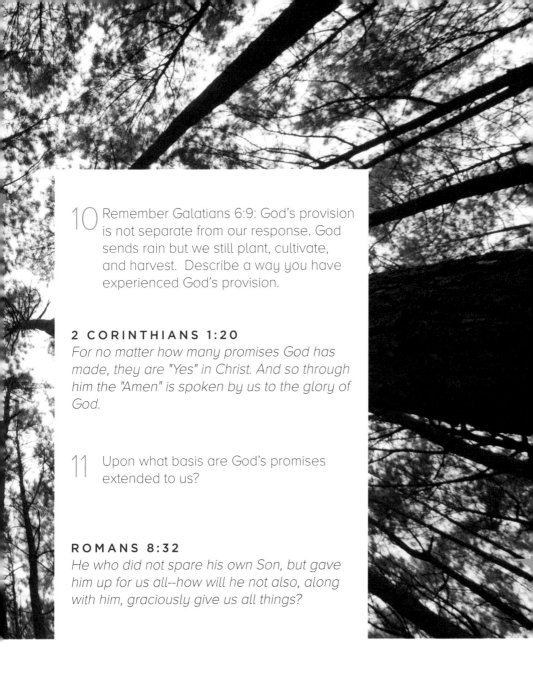

10 Remember Galatians 6:9: God's provision is not separate from our response. God sends rain but we still plant, cultivate, and harvest. Describe a way you have experienced God's provision.

2 CORINTHIANS 1:20
For no matter how many promises God has made, they are "Yes" in Christ. And so through him the "Amen" is spoken by us to the glory of God.

11 Upon what basis are God's promises extended to us?

ROMANS 8:32
He who did not spare his own Son, but gave him up for us all--how will he not also, along with him, graciously give us all things?

God's provision for us was made through Jesus' sacrifice. When we refuse to believe or accept God's provision, we are rejecting Jesus. Unbelief is not a position of humility and sacrifice; it is a posture of pride and rebellion. Trust and faithfulness are responses of possibility because of Who God is. Intentionally lay down skepticism and unbelief and pick up trust. The outcome will be good.

12 Take a moment and list some spiritual blessings God has made available to you through Jesus' redemptive work. (Hint: 1. Righteousness)

PHILIPPIANS 4:12-13
¹² I know what it is to be in need, and I know what it is to have plenty. I have learned the secret of being content in any and every situation, whether well fed or hungry, whether living in plenty or in want. ¹³ I can do everything through him who gives me strength.

13 Describe a season when your resources were less but your contentment/joy were not diminished.

HEBREWS 12:26-29
²⁶ . . . but now he has promised, "Once more I will shake not only the earth but also the heavens." ²⁷ The words "once more" indicate the removing of what can be shaken--that is, created things--so that what cannot be shaken may remain. ²⁸ Therefore, since we are receiving a kingdom that cannot be shaken, let us be thankful, and so worship God acceptably with reverence and awe, ²⁹ for our "God is a consuming fire."

14 Who is the source of shaking? What will be shaken?

Seasons of less are a part of life's journey. They are not an expression of failure or God's displeasure. Uncertainty is a certain part of our future for God is shaking the earth. The result is the unshakeable Kingdom of God, which will be increasingly apparent. The Holy Spirit will help us to grow in faith and to escape the deception of "self security" as we learn to trust in God and His abundance.

15 As you close, take a few minutes to discuss areas where you would like to trust God more completely.

Prayer

Close the session by reading this prayer together. Make it your prayer each day in the coming week.

Heavenly Father, I rejoice in Your abundant provision of grace for my life. I lay aside my fear and reluctance to respond in praise and thanksgiving. You are a faithful God, a God of power and compassion. I will trust in You. My future is secure because my God is able. Grant me the strength to complete the course You have ordained for me. Open the eyes of my understanding to recognize Your invitations. Thank You for Your loving provision of abundance. In Jesus' name, amen.

PRAYER REQUEST

Additional Study

Each week's lesson is built to be self-contained. However, some like to prepare in advance for the next session. If this is you, visit us online for Pastor Allen's full sermon on each session as well as other tools for additional study in preparation for next week.

To prepare for next week, watch

Fullness of His Provision

TheMostAbundantLife.com

Daily Devotions

Day 1
The World

For this world in its present form is passing away.

1 CORINTHIANS 7:31

Day 2
Choose the Best

²² If I am to go on living in the body, this will mean fruitful labor for me. Yet what shall I choose? I do not know! ²³ I am torn between the two: I desire to depart and be with Christ, which is better by far; ²⁴ but it is more necessary for you that I remain in the body.

PHILIPPIANS 1:22-24

Day 3
Uncertainty and Shaking

⁷ Nation will rise up against nation, and kingdom against kingdom. There will be famines and earthquakes in various places. ⁸ All these are the beginning of birth pains.

MATTHEW 24:7-8

reflection question:

In what ways can you see this world passing away?

reflection question:

Consider the people who make it necessary for you to remain in the body.

reflection question:

How does knowing God's character prepare you as these days approach?

Memory Verse

2 Peter 1:3 — *His divine power has given us everything we need for a godly life through our knowledge of him who called us by his own glory and goodness.*

Day 4
Choose Right

But the worries of this life, the deceitfulness of wealth and the desires for other things come in and choke the word, making it unfruitful.

MARK 4:19

Day 5
Provision

His divine power has given us everything we need for a godly life through our knowledge of him who called us by his own glory and goodness.

2 PETER 1:3

reflection question:

Think about the ways you can invest in the Kingdom of God that will have lasting rewards to help you avoid this warning.

reflection question:

How much has God provided for you? Why has He provided it?

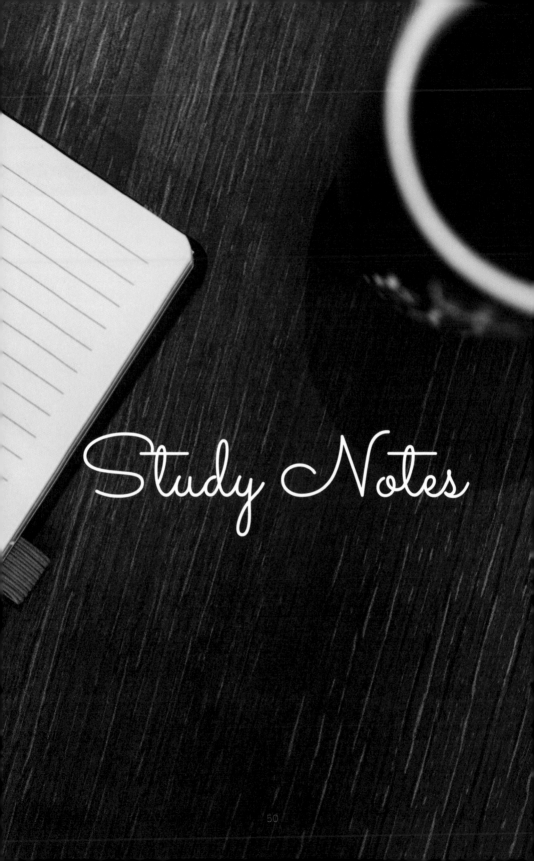

Study Notes

03

Fullness of His Provision

As Christ-followers, we can live courageously in seasons that bring fear to many. God's provision for us is about His depth of resources, not ours. In fact, in our weakness, the strength of God is even more evident. We are growing in trust and faithfulness. Serving the Lord is the most exciting life possible.

getting

→ Begin your time together by using one or both of the following icebreakers.

Share your favorite season and why.

Tell a favorite summer camp memory.

started

Outline of DVD Lesson

Use the outline below to follow along during the DVD. The answers to the blanks below can be found in the video.

GENESIS 8:22

"As long as the earth endures, seedtime and harvest, cold and heat, summer and winter, day and night will never cease."

God is the one who oversees the _____ of our lives.

I. The Abundance of God—in time & eternity

A. In Time—Fullness of His Provision

PSALM 84:11

For the LORD God is a sun and shield; the LORD bestows favor and honor; no good thing does he withhold from those whose walk is blameless.

God doesn't withhold any _____ thing from you.

Your value is _____ established by wealth.

B. In Eternity—Glory of His Kingdom

MATTHEW 25:31-32
31 *"When the Son of Man comes in his glory, and all the angels with him, he will sit on his throne in heavenly glory. 32 All the nations will be gathered before him, and he will separate the people one from another as a shepherd separates the sheep from the goats."*

II. God Is Our Source

A. Abundance Is a Blessing

DEUTERONOMY 28:11
The LORD will grant you abundant prosperity—in the fruit of your womb, the young of your livestock and the crops of your ground—in the land he swore to your forefathers to give you.

_____ *is a blessing from God.*

B. Poverty, a Curse

DEUTERONOMY 28:47-48 (NASB)
47 *"Because you did not serve the LORD your God with joy and a glad heart, for the abundance of all things; 48 therefore you shall serve your*

enemies whom the LORD will send against you, in hunger, in thirst, in nakedness, and in the lack of all things . . . "

_____ *is a curse.*

III. Adjusting our Thoughts and Attitudes

ROMANS 12:2
Do not conform any longer to the pattern of this world, but be transformed by the renewing of your mind. Then you will be able to test and approve what God's will is—his good, pleasing and perfect will.

    A. 3 Successive Stages to Understanding God's Will:

        1. It's good.
        2. It's pleasing.
        3. It's perfect/complete.

The will of God is for your _____ *life.*

    B. God's Intent

3 JOHN 1:2 (NASB)
Beloved, I pray that in all respects you may prosper and be in good health, just as your soul prospers.

Three areas: good _____*, soul, and resources.*

God's desire is that His people would _____.

Failure, defeat, frustration, and poverty are not the will of God.

Answers: harvest; good; not; prosperity; poverty; complete; health; prosper

58

The grass withers and the flowers fall, but the word of our God endures forever.

Isaiah 40:8

Discussion

Using the questions that follow, we will review and expand on the DVD presentation.

READ ALOUD

God does not want to take good things away from you. Just the opposite is true. God's desire is to add good things to your life. We learn from the Bible that every person is valuable to God— He loves every one of us. Our value is not established by our appearance, our intellect, or our wealth. Our value is established by God's love for us. The Creator of the universe, Almighty God, says we are significant. Romans 8:31 reminds us, "If God is for us, who can be against us?"

PSALM 84:11
For the LORD God is a sun and shield; the LORD bestows favor and honor; no good thing does he withhold from those whose walk is blameless.

1   To withhold is stated in the negative; to release is the positive. Describe a time God released a blessing into your life.

DEUTERONOMY 28:11
The LORD will grant you abundant prosperity—in the fruit of your womb, the young of your livestock and the crops of your ground—in the land he swore to your forefathers to give you.

DEUTERONOMY 8:18
But remember the LORD your God, for it is he who gives you the ability to produce wealth, and so confirms his covenant, which he swore to your forefathers, as it is today.

2   Who does Scripture teach us grants us prosperity and the opportunity to accumulate resources?

3   Why do we often imagine God does not want us to have good things?

DEUTERONOMY 28:47-48 (NASB)
47 "Because you did not serve the LORD your God with joy and a glad heart, for the abundance of all things; 48 therefore you shall serve your enemies whom the LORD will send against you, in hunger, in thirst, in nakedness, and in the lack of all things . . . "

4   Refusing to serve the Lord is a life apart from God. What is the outcome of a life apart from God?

Application

Now it is time to make some personal applications of all we have been thinking about in the last few minutes.

READ ALOUD

The contrast between a life with God (enjoying His blessing) and a life apart from God is very clear. Yet we often struggle to believe godliness is better. We try to create the benefits of godliness without yielding to God—it does not work. It is far wiser to cooperate with God and receive the blessings of our Heavenly Father.

5   We do not earn God's abundance—we receive it. Describe a time you were able to believe God and the outcome was positive.

ROMANS 12:2

Do not conform any longer to the pattern of this world, but be transformed by the renewing of your mind. Then you will be able to test and approve what God's will is--his good, pleasing and perfect will.

6   To be transformed is to be changed in potential. How is our potential changed?

7   Describe a new way of thinking that has emerged from trusting the Lord.

8   What three words are used to describe God's will?

READ ALOUD

God's will is good—it is good for you and will result in good. God's will is pleasing. If you do not want to do God's will, you do not understand it fully. When understood, God's will is pleasing. God's will is perfect and complete. God has a plan for your complete life. Combined, this is an amazing revelation regarding our God. His will for us is good, pleasing, and includes our complete life.

9   In what part of your life is God's will easiest to cooperate with? The most difficult?

EXODUS 20:17

"You shall not covet your neighbor's house. You shall not covet your neighbor's wife, or his manservant or maidservant, his ox or donkey, or anything that belongs to your neighbor."

1 TIMOTHY 6:6

But godliness with contentment is great gain.

10 There is a tension between "wanting more" and contentment. Describe one arena in which you have discovered the benefit of contentment.

11 How has godliness contributed to contentment in your life?

12 Acquisition and accumulation do not bring contentment. Identify an area of discontent in your life and discuss what increased godliness in that area might look like.

READ ALOUD

God wants good things for our lives. His blessings bring abundance and contentment. Poverty, failure, defeat, frustration, and despair are not God's intent for His children. We may endure seasons of less, but we can know God's desire is to lead us through these times. Learning God's intent regarding our resources is an important part of our spiritual growth. It is prudent to seek God's opinion about your money. He wants good things for you.

13 What does God's abundance look like in your life?

14 Discuss the most recent good things God has provided for you.

Prayer

Close the session by reading this prayer together. Make it your prayer each day in the coming week.

Heavenly Father, grant me an understanding heart that I might know Your will. Teach me to order my steps that Your very best might fill my life. I believe You desire good things for me. I yield all that I have to the Lordship of Jesus of Nazareth—my time, my talent, my strength, and my resources. I offer myself as a living sacrifice. I rejoice in the security of my God. I dwell under the shadow of Your protection. May Your peace watch over my mind and emotions. In Jesus' name, amen.

PRAYER REQUEST

Additional Study

Each week's lesson is built to be self-contained. However, some like to prepare in advance for the next session. If this is you, visit us online for Pastor Allen's full sermon on each session as well as other tools for additional study in preparation for next week.

To prepare for next week, watch

Total Security

TheMostAbundantLife.com

Daily Devotions

Day 1
Seek First

³¹ "So do not worry, saying, 'What shall we eat?' or 'What shall we drink?' or 'What shall we wear?' ³² For the pagans run after all these things, and your heavenly Father knows that you need them. ³³ But seek first his kingdom and his righteousness, and all these things will be given to you as well."

MATTHEW 6:31-33

reflection question:

What are some ways you can put into practice seeking His kingdom and righteousness?

Day 2
Firmly Planted

² . . . but whose delight is in the law of the Lord, and who meditates on his law day and night. ³ That person is like a tree planted by streams of water, which yields its fruit in season and whose leaf does not wither—whatever they do prospers.

PSALM 1:2-3

reflection question:

Today, do you feel well-nourished or depleted?

Day 3
Serve with Joy

² Serve the LORD with gladness: come before his presence with singing. ³ Know ye that the LORD he is God: it is he that hath made us, and not we ourselves; we are his people, and the sheep of his pasture.

PSALM 100:2-3 (KJV)

reflection question:

Is it easy for you to serve the Lord with enthusiasm and gladness, or is this difficult for you? Take a minute and ask the Lord to help you have a servant's heart.

Memory Verse

Isaiah 40:8 — *"The grass withers and the flowers fall, but the word of our God endures forever."*

Day 4
Peace and Security

"'Nevertheless, I will bring health and healing to it; I will heal my people and will let them enjoy abundant peace and security.'"

Day 5
Enduring Word

"The grass withers and the flowers fall, but the word of our God endures forever."

JEREMIAH 33:6

ISAIAH 40:8

---

reflection question:

Spend the day thanking God for His abundant peace and security.

reflection question:

There is great security in knowing the Word of God is infallible and enduring. How much time are you currently investing in Bible reading?

Study Notes

04

Total Security

We are exploring together God's provision for our abundant life. Almighty God is interested in our well-being. Knowing God and His provision enables us to live fearlessly, even in frightening seasons. Our security and strength are anchored in the eternal, unchanging character of God. Through God's Word, we can understand God's will and purpose. It is a marvelous privilege to rest in the protective shadow of the God of Abraham, Isaac, and Jacob.

getting

→ Begin your time together by using one or both of the following icebreakers.

Share your best memory of the house you grew up in.

Do you have a nickname?

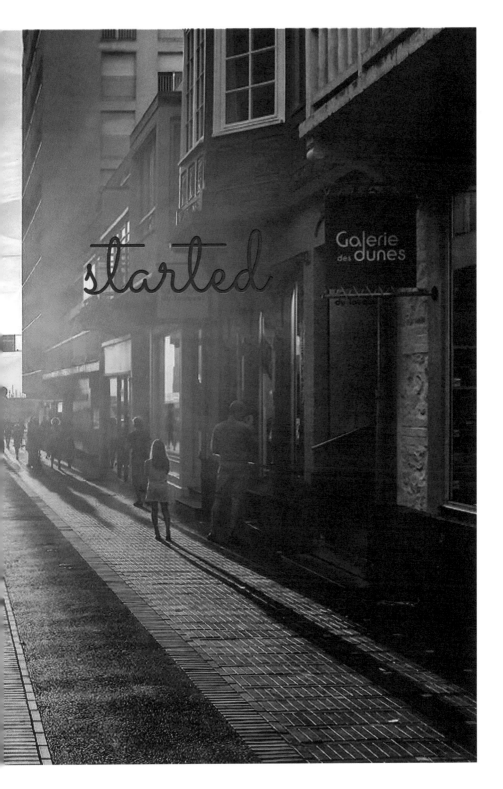

Outline of DVD Lesson

Use the outline below to follow along during the DVD. The answers to the blanks below can be found in the video.

I. God's Complete Provision

There is _____ halfway about God.

NEHEMIAH 9:17, 19-22

[17] *"They refused to listen and failed to remember the miracles you performed among them. . . .* [19] *Because of your great compassion you did not abandon them in the desert. By day the pillar of cloud did not cease to guide them on their path, nor the pillar of fire by night to shine on the way they were to take.* [20] *You gave your good Spirit to instruct them. You did not withhold your manna from their mouths, and you gave them water for their thirst.* [21] *For forty years you sustained them in the desert; they lacked nothing, their clothes did not wear out nor did their feet become swollen.* [22] *You gave them kingdoms and nations, allotting to them even the remotest frontiers."*

II. God's Provision in His Promises

2 PETER 1:3-4

[3] *His divine power has given us everything we need for life and godliness through our knowledge of him who called us by his own glory and goodness.* [4] *Through these he has given us his very great and precious promises, so that through them you may participate in the divine nature and escape the corruption in the world caused by evil desires.*

God's provision for you and me is in His _____.

III. Revelation and Provision

Provision emerges from a _____ of God.

How you know God _____ much about His provision in your life.

A. The Son's Perspective

HEBREWS 1:1-2
¹ In the past God spoke to our forefathers through the prophets at many times and in various ways, ² but in these last days he has spoken to us by his Son, whom he appointed heir of all things, and through whom he made the universe.

Jesus can help us know God as _____.

B. Knowing the Father

JOHN 14:6-7

6 Jesus answered, "I am the way and the truth and the life. No one comes to the Father except through me. 7 If you really knew me, you would know my Father as well. From now on, you do know him and have seen him."

C. God Is Our Father

MATTHEW 6:9-13 (NASB)

9 "Pray, then, in this way:
'Our Father who is in heaven, Hallowed be Your name.
10 'Your kingdom come. Your will be done, On earth as it is in heaven.
11 'Give us this day our daily bread.
12 'And forgive us our debts, as we also have forgiven our debtors.
13 'And do not lead us into temptation, but deliver us from evil. For Yours is the kingdom and the power and the glory forever. Amen.'"

The heart of Jesus' message is to know _____ as Father.

D. Knowing the Father

EPHESIANS 1:6 (KJV)

To the praise of the glory of his grace, wherein he hath made us accepted in the beloved.

God has _____ us!

LUKE 12:32-33

32 "Do not be afraid, little flock, for your Father has been pleased to give you the kingdom. 33 Sell your possessions and give to the poor. Provide purses for yourselves that will not wear out, a treasure in heaven that will not be exhausted, where no thief comes near and no moth destroys."

Answers: nothing; promises; revelation; determines; Father; God; accepted

To the praise of the glory of his grace, wherein he hath made us accepted in the beloved.

Ephesians 1:6 (KJV)

Discussion

Using the questions that follow, we will review and expand on the teaching we just experienced.

READ ALOUD

Jesus encouraged us to cultivate a childlike faith. Children have a remarkable trust and confidence in their parents. Jesus trusted His Father in heaven. It is common to wrestle with God's provision. We learn to trust Him.

1   As we learn to trust God we can live fearlessly, even in frightening times. What are some of the greatest fears you confront?

NEHEMIAH 9:17, 19-22

" *17 They refused to listen and failed to remember the miracles you performed among them. . . . 19 Because of your great compassion you did not abandon them in the desert. By day the pillar of cloud did not cease to guide them on their path, nor the pillar of fire by night to shine on the way they were to take. 20 You gave your good Spirit to instruct them. You did not withhold your manna from their mouths, and you gave them water for their thirst. 21 For forty years you sustained them in the desert; they lacked nothing, their clothes did not wear out nor did their feet become swollen. 22 You gave them kingdoms and nations, allotting to them even the remotest frontiers."*

2   Nehemiah lists seven specific ways God provided for the Hebrews on their desert journey. List them.

3   What was the response of the people to God's abundant provision?

HEBREWS 3:12-13

12 *See to it, brothers, that none of you has a sinful, unbelieving heart that turns away from the living God.* 13 *But encourage one another daily, as long as it is called Today, so that none of you may be hardened by sin's deceitfulness.*

4   What is one provision that enables us to not turn away from God?

5   Describe a time when someone's encouragement enabled you to persevere.

Application

Now it is time to make some personal applications of all we have been thinking about in the last few minutes.

READ ALOUD
In the New Covenant, God's provision is in His promises. To the Hebrew people, God promised an inheritance of "The Promised Land." We have the privilege of living in the abundance of God's promises. Our inheritance is in the promises of God.

2 PETER 1:3-4

³ His divine power has given us everything we need for life and godliness through our knowledge of him who called us by his own glory and goodness.
⁴ Through these he has given us his very great and precious promises, so that through them you may participate in the divine nature and escape the corruption in the world caused by evil desires.

6 What has God's divine power given to us?

7 Discuss which seem more challenging—the needs of life or the needs of godliness.

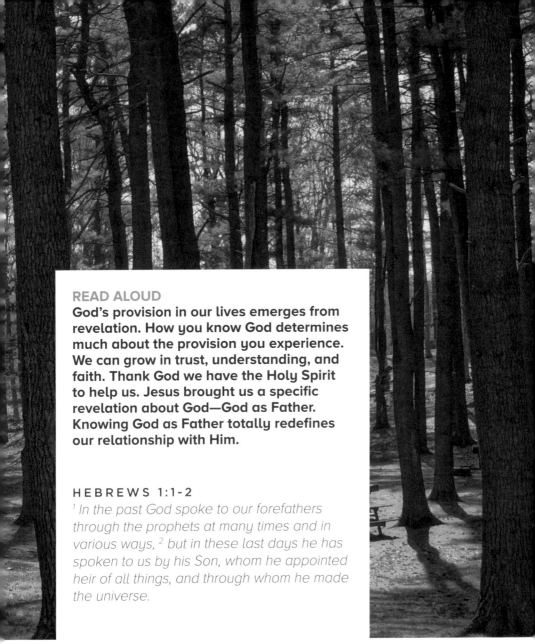

God's provision in our lives emerges from revelation. How you know God determines much about the provision you experience. We can grow in trust, understanding, and faith. Thank God we have the Holy Spirit to help us. Jesus brought us a specific revelation about God—God as Father. Knowing God as Father totally redefines our relationship with Him.

HEBREWS 1:1-2

[1] In the past God spoke to our forefathers through the prophets at many times and in various ways, [2] but in these last days he has spoken to us by his Son, whom he appointed heir of all things, and through whom he made the universe.

8 In verse 2, we discover two things about Jesus. List them.

JOHN 14:6-7

⁶ *Jesus answered, "I am the way and the truth and the life. No one comes to the Father except through me. ⁷ If you really knew me, you would know my Father as well. From now on, you do know him and have seen him."*

MATTHEW 6:9-13 (NASB)

⁹ *"Pray, then, in this way:*
'Our Father who is in heaven, Hallowed be Your name.
¹⁰ *'Your kingdom come. Your will be done, On earth as it is in heaven.*
¹¹ *'Give us this day our daily bread.*
¹² *'And forgive us our debts, as we also have forgiven our debtors.*
¹³ *'And do not lead us into temptation, but deliver us from evil. For Yours is the kingdom and the power and the glory forever. Amen.'"*

READ ALOUD

Jesus gave us a revelation—God is our Father. We can approach God as His children, trusting His provision, protection, and discipline. At the heart of the revelation of God as our Father is acceptance. God has accepted us. We are not alone, abandoned, or rejected. He has made provision for our failures and weaknesses. He has welcomed us into His kingdom as His children. We have a home in eternity and the watchful care of Almighty God over our lives in time.

9   What are the responsibilities of a good father?

10   How do the responsibilities of a father change as he matures?

11   What are your responsibilities toward your earthly father?

2 PETER 1:3

His divine power has given us everything we need for life and godliness through our knowledge of him who called us by his own glory and goodness.

12 How does this verse change the revelation of God as your Father?

13 Trust is the antidote to fear. Discuss ways you would like to learn to trust God more completely.

Prayer

Close the session by reading this prayer together. Make it your prayer each day in the coming week.

Heavenly Father, thank You for accepting me as Your child. I rejoice in Your great provision for my life. You have not withheld any good thing from me. You have made extravagant provision for my life in time and eternity. Help me to learn to trust You more. I lay aside worry and fear and take up the garment of praise and thanksgiving. I will lift my heart and my voice in worship to the Maker of heaven and earth. In Jesus I have found redemption, forgiveness, acceptance, and an inheritance. In His name I rejoice and offer this prayer, amen.

PRAYER REQUEST

Additional Study

Each week's lesson is built to be self-contained. However, some like to prepare in advance for the next session. If this is you, visit us online for Pastor Allen's full sermon on each session as well as other tools for additional study in preparation for next week.

To prepare for next week, watch

The Experience Key

TheMostAbundantLife.com

Daily Devotions

Day 1
Life Surrendered

Anyone who loves their life will lose it, while anyone who hates their life in this world will keep it for eternal life.

JOHN 12:25

Day 2
Father of All

25 There is the sea, vast and spacious, teeming with creatures beyond number—living things both large and small... 27 All creatures look to you to give them their food at the proper time.

PSALM 104:25, 27

Day 3
Accepted by God

To the praise of the glory of his grace, wherein he hath made us accepted in the beloved.

EPHESIANS 1:6 (KJV)

reflection question:

Recall a time you relinquished your desire and will to God's will for your life. What was the outcome?

reflection question:

Do you feel free to call God, Father? Take a minute and begin to thank Him that He is your Father.

reflection question:

Can you remember a time when you did not feel accepted? Take a moment and tell the Lord you forgive that person or persons.

Memory Verse

Ephesians 1:6 (KJV) — *To the praise of the glory of his grace, wherein he hath made us accepted in the beloved.*

Day 4
Home in Heaven

"My Father's house has many rooms; if that were not so, would I have told you that I am going there to prepare a place for you?"

JOHN 14:2

Day 5
Not Alone

"The one who sent me is with me; he has not left me alone, for I always do what pleases him."

JOHN 8:29

---

reflection question:

God is making preparations for you. How are you preparing for Him today?

reflection question:

Say the above Scripture as a proclamation for today!

Study Notes

05

The Experience Key

Our objective in this study is to participate in God's provision for our most abundant life. Understanding God as our Source enables us to live fearlessly, even in frightening seasons. In this session, we will explore the choices that unlock God's response to us. We want to experience God, not just have discussions about what He might do.

getting

 Begin your time together by using one or both of the following icebreakers.

In one word, how do you want to be remembered?

Was there anything you recognized this week as God's abundance?

started

Outline of DVD Lesson

Use the outline below to follow along during the DVD. The answers to the blanks below can be found in the video.

I. Experiencing God

JOHN 20:27
Then he said to Thomas, "Put your finger here; see my hands. Reach out your hand and put it into my side. Stop doubting and believe."

Truth divorced from _____ must always dwell in the realm of doubt.

    A. Experience Redemption

ROMANS 10:9-10
[9] If you confess with your mouth, "Jesus is Lord," and believe in your heart that God raised him from the dead, you will be saved. [10] For it is with your heart that you believe and are justified, and it is with your mouth that you confess and are saved.

    B. Experience Forgiveness

1 JOHN 1:8-9
[8] If we claim to be without sin, we deceive ourselves and the truth is not in us. [9] If we confess our sins, he is faithful and just and will forgive us our sins and purify us from all unrighteousness.

If we refuse to forgive, we _____ something.

These keys _____ the benefit of God's abundant provision.

C. Experience Mercy

MATTHEW 5:7
Blessed are the merciful, for they will be shown mercy.

Your Response: Give mercy—receive _____.

D. Experience Summation

LUKE 6:37-38
[37] "Do not judge, and you will not be judged. Do not condemn, and you will not be condemned. Forgive, and you will be forgiven. [38] Give, and it will be given to you. A good measure, pressed down, shaken together and running over, will be poured into your lap. For with the measure you use, it will be measured to you."

Do not judge—express grace	=	receive no judgment
Do not condemn—show mercy	=	receive no condemnation
Do not hold unforgiveness—forgive	=	receive forgiveness
Do not covet—give	=	receive abundance

II. God's Level of Provision

2 CORINTHIANS 9:6-8

⁶ Remember this: Whoever sows sparingly will also reap sparingly, and whoever sows generously will also reap generously. ⁷ Each man should give what he has decided in his heart to give, not reluctantly or under compulsion, for God loves a cheerful giver. ⁸ And God is able to make all grace abound to you, so that in all things at all times, having all that you need, you will abound in every good work.

_____ *Things*

_____ *Times*

_____ *You Need*

= *Abundance*

Answers: experience; forfeit; unlock; mercy; all; all; all

He who did not spare his own Son,
but gave him up for us all—how will he
not also, along with him, graciously give
us all things?

Romans 8:32

Discussion

Using the questions that follow, we will review and expand on the teaching we just experienced.

READ ALOUD

Confidence grows when your ideas are supported by experience. You can read one hundred books about watermelon, but the experience of eating watermelon is far more powerful than another book. We often settle for a study about spiritual truth and miss the experience. Your faith will grow as you experience the power of God when you cooperate with His truth.

JOHN 20:24-25

24 Now Thomas (called Didymus), one of the Twelve, was not with the disciples when Jesus came. 25 So the other disciples told him, "We have seen the Lord!" But he said to them, "Unless I see the nail marks in his hands and put my finger where the nails were, and put my hand into his side, I will not believe it."

1   Why was Thomas reluctant to believe the report from the other disciples?

JOHN 20:26-29

26 A week later his disciples were in the house again, and Thomas was with them. Though the doors were locked, Jesus came and stood among them and said, "Peace be with you!" 27 Then he said to Thomas, "Put your finger here; see my hands. Reach out your hand and put it into my side. Stop doubting and believe." 28 Thomas said to him, "My Lord and my God!" 29 Then Jesus told him, "Because you have seen me, you have believed; blessed are those who have not seen and yet have believed."

2   What was Jesus' objective in the invitation He extended to Thomas?

3   How long did Thomas have to wait before he saw Jesus?

4   What feelings do you suppose Thomas struggled with during those days? What would the discussions with other disciples have been like?

5   Have you experienced God in a way that strengthened your belief? Explain.

6   Describe an occasion when you were reluctant to believe, even when others encouraged you to take a step of faith.

Application

Now it is time to make some personal applications of all we have been thinking about in the last few minutes.

READ ALOUD

There are keys to experiencing God's provision for our lives. We cannot ignore the directions of the Creator and experience God's abundant provision. Frequently, we struggle with yielding to God. Instead, we offer our thoughts, our suggestions, our impressions while we are reluctant to accept God's direction. Obedience is a powerful choice.

Redemption

ROMANS 10:9-10

⁹ If you confess with your mouth, "Jesus is Lord," and believe in your heart that God raised him from the dead, you will be saved. ¹⁰ For it is with your heart that you believe and are justified, and it is with your mouth that you confess and are saved.

7 What is required to be saved?

8 If you refuse to acknowledge Jesus is Lord, is Jesus diminished?

God's provision for us was completed with Jesus' death and resurrection. Your experience takes place when you believe and act. Your faith in action unlocks the benefit. If you fail to believe and respond, the benefit is forfeited.

Forgiveness

1 JOHN 1:8-9

⁸ If we claim to be without sin, we deceive ourselves and the truth is not in us. ⁹ If we confess our sins, he is faithful and just and will forgive us our sins and purify us from all unrighteousness.

MATTHEW 6:14-15

¹⁴ For if you forgive men when they sin against you, your heavenly Father will also forgive you. ¹⁵ But if you do not forgive men their sins, your Father will not forgive your sins.

9   What are the experience keys for receiving forgiveness from God?

    a. acknowledge our need for forgiveness
    b. confess, ask for forgiveness
    c. _____

10   Can forgiveness from God be achieved in another way—through serving others, generosity, personal piety?

Abundance

2 CORINTHIANS 9:6-8

6 Remember this: Whoever sows sparingly will also reap sparingly, and whoever sows generously will also reap generously. 7 Each man should give what he has decided in his heart to give, not reluctantly or under compulsion, for God loves a cheerful giver. 8 And God is able to make all grace abound to you, so that in all things at all times, having all that you need, you will abound in every good work.

READ ALOUD
This passage extends an amazing promise of abundance—all things, at all times, having all that you need to abound in every good work. Almighty God has promised abundance in our lives. It is His provision for us.

11   What is the experience key to receiving God's abundance?

12   Why are Christ-followers sometimes reluctant to "give generously"?

13 What do we forfeit when we give sparingly?

READ ALOUD
God presents us with a choice. We can choose our own path to achieve abundance or we can accept His counsel and experience God's most abundant life. Following God's path is often a challenge; it requires faith, obedience, and the encouragement of others.

14 Take a moment and share a part of your own journey in learning to give—the struggles and the benefits.

Prayer

Close the session by reading this prayer together. Make it your prayer each day in the coming week.

Heavenly Father, thank You for Your abundant provision for my life. Through Jesus, You have made available complete salvation. Open the eyes of my heart to Your truth. I choose obedience to You. I choose to forgive that I may be forgiven. I choose to live generously that I may experience Your provision. I rejoice in the grace and mercy of my God and His most abundant provision for my life. In Jesus' name, amen.

PRAYER REQUEST

Additional Study

Each week's lesson is built to be self-contained. However, some like to prepare in advance for the next session. If this is you, visit us online for Pastor Allen's full sermon on each session as well as other tools for additional study in preparation for next week.

To prepare for next week, watch

The Blessings of Generosity

Daily Devotions

Day 1
Forgiveness

For if you forgive men when they sin against you, your heavenly Father will also forgive you.

MATTHEW 6:14

Day 2
Gave It All

He who did not spare his own Son, but gave him up for us all--how will he not also, along with him, graciously give us all things?

ROMANS 8:32

Day 3
Believe

Then he said to Thomas, "Put your finger here; see my hands. Reach out your hand and put it into my side. Stop doubting and believe."

JOHN 20:27

reflection question:

Does anyone come to mind who you could choose to forgive today?

reflection question:

List some of the blessings that God has showered on your life.

reflection question:

What one thing can you choose to believe God for today?

Memory Verse

Romans 8:32 — *He who did not spare his own Son, but gave him up for us all--how will he not also, along with him, graciously give us all things?*

Day 4
Provision

Now he who supplies seed to the sower and bread for food will also supply and increase your store of seed and will enlarge the harvest of your righteousness.

2 CORINTHIANS 9:10

Day 5
Seeking

But seek first his kingdom and his righteousness, and all these things will be given to you as well.

MATTHEW 6:33

reflection question:

Spend time today thanking God for His provision.

reflection question:

Seeking His Kingdom requires knowing Him in a new way. What can you begin today that would help you know Him better?

Study Notes

06

The Blessings of Generosity

Generosity is not a burden; it is an opportunity. We have spent several weeks asking God for a revelation of His abundance for us. The session this week presents us with a practical way to ignite a life of God's abundance. The principles are not complex. The implementation often generates an internal struggle. Do not be surprised if this is true for you. A response of faith always emerges from a struggle within. Faith says "yes" to God's invitation.

getting

→ Begin your time together by using one or both of the following icebreakers.

What is the best gift you have ever received?

What is the best gift you have ever given?

started

Outline of DVD Lesson

Use the outline below to follow along during the DVD. The answers to the blanks below can be found in the video.

I. The Power of Giving

LUKE 6:38
"Give, and it will be given to you. A good measure, pressed down, shaken together and running over, will be poured into your lap. For with the measure you use, it will be measured to you."

Giving makes us _____ in God's responses to our lives.

We cannot buy favor from God. He does not need anything from us.

Good parents teach their children to manage money.

God wants to help His _____ learn about money too!

A. Is Giving Arbitrary?

EXODUS 12:3,5
[3] *"Tell the whole community of Israel that on the tenth day of this month each man is to take a lamb for his family, one for each household . . .*
[5] *The animals you choose must be year-old males without defect, and you may take them from the sheep or the goats."*

GENESIS 4:2-7

2 Later she gave birth to his brother Abel. Now Abel kept flocks, and Cain worked the soil. 3 In the course of time Cain brought some of the fruits of the soil as an offering to the LORD. 4 But Abel brought fat portions from some of the firstborn of his flock. The LORD looked with favor on Abel and his offering, 5 but on Cain and his offering he did not look with favor. So Cain was very angry, and his face was downcast. 6 Then the LORD said to Cain, "Why are you angry? Why is your face downcast? 7 If you do what is right, will you not be accepted? But if you do not do what is right, sin is crouching at your door; it desires to have you, but you must master it."

B. Giving as Worship

MALACHI 3:8-11 (NASB)

8 "Will a man rob God? Yet you are robbing Me! But you say, 'How have we robbed You?' In tithes and offerings. 9 You are cursed with a curse, for you are robbing Me, the whole nation of you! 10 Bring the whole tithe into the storehouse, so that there may be food in My house, and test Me now in this," says the LORD of hosts, "if I will not open for you the windows of heaven and pour out for you a blessing until it overflows. 11 Then I will rebuke the devourer for you, so that it will not destroy the fruits of the ground; nor will your vine in the field cast its grapes," says the LORD of hosts.

Giving is an experience key to God's
_____.

II. Money Matters

A. Warnings

1. Greed

LUKE 12:15 (NASB)
Then He said to them, "Beware, and be on your guard against every form of greed; for not even when one has an abundance does his life consist of his possessions."

Greed is _____.

2. Laziness

2 THESSALONIANS 3:10
For even when we were with you, we gave you this rule: "If a man will not work, he shall not eat."

_____ *is an expression of godliness.*

3. Deceitfulness of Wealth

MATTHEW 13:22
"The one who received the seed that fell among the thorns is the man who hears the word, but the worries of this life and the deceitfulness of wealth choke it, making it unfruitful."

Money can _____ *us.*

B. Encouraged

    1. Generous

PROVERBS 11:25
A generous man will prosper; he who refreshes others will himself be refreshed.

Practice _____.

    2. Accumulate (true) Wealth

1 TIMOTHY 6:17-19
[17] *Command those who are rich in this present world not to be arrogant nor to put their hope in wealth, which is so uncertain, but to put their hope in God, who richly provides us with everything for our enjoyment.*
[18] *Command them to do good, to be rich in good deeds, and to be generous and willing to share.* [19] *In this way they will lay up treasure for themselves as a firm foundation for the coming age, so that they may take hold of the life that is truly life.*

A generous man will prosper; he who refreshes others will himself be refreshed.

Proverbs 11:25

Answers: participants; children; abundance; disruptive; work; deceive; generosity

Discussion

Using the questions that follow, we will review and expand on the teaching we just experienced.

READ ALOUD

Giving unleashes a spiritual force. Generosity is not a neutral response. It is an expression of faith. We want to intentionally develop our "muscles of generosity." The outcome is a better life.

1   Identify ways you can give generously with something other than money.

2   Describe a time you received a non-monetary gift—forgiveness, kindness, assistance, listening, etc.—and the benefit that you recognized.

READ ALOUD

Planting is a declaration of faith. We plant flowers in full anticipation of flowers. When we plant corn, we are expecting corn. These responses are not presumptuous. There are risks— weather, insects, animals—but the anticipated reward is more enticing than the risks are daunting. We practice generosity in faith, knowing the outcome is often challenged but realizing God is overseeing all.

LUKE 6:38

"Give, and it will be given to you. A good measure, pressed down, shaken together and running over, will be poured into your lap. For with the measure you use, it will be measured to you."

3   What determines God's level of response to you?

4   If you refuse to be generous, what does that imply for the season ahead?

LUKE 21:1-4

¹ As he looked up, Jesus saw the rich putting their gifts into the temple treasury. ² He also saw a poor widow put in two very small copper coins. ³ "I tell you the truth," he said, "this poor widow has put in more than all the others. ⁴ All these people gave their gifts out of their wealth; but she out of her poverty put in all she had to live on."

5   Why does Jesus commend the widow for generosity?

Application

Now it is time to make some personal applications of all we have been thinking about in the last few minutes.

READ ALOUD
You cannot buy favor from God. He does not need anything from us. The biblical directions toward generosity are for our benefit. God wants to help His children learn about abundance. In a similar fashion, parents teach their children about money and its value. God provides direction so that His people may lead abundant lives.

EXODUS 12:3,5

³ *"Tell the whole community of Israel that on the tenth day of this month each man is to take a lamb for his family, one for each household . . .* ⁵ *The animals you choose must be year-old males without defect, and you may take them from the sheep or the goats."*

GENESIS 4:4-5

⁴ *. . . the LORD looked with favor on Abel and his offering,* ⁵ *but on Cain and his offering he did not look with favor. So Cain was very angry, and his face was downcast.*

6   Is giving arbitrary, based on personal inclination, or has God provided direction?

7 Cain was angry. Why does the thought of God directing generosity sometimes result in resentment? Have you experienced a similar response?

READ ALOUD
God provides direction on forgiveness, honoring our parents, and even sexuality. We cannot arbitrarily decide which truth to obey and imagine God's full blessings upon our lives. God implemented the idea of a tithe—a tenth—as an expression of worship. God does not want to diminish us; He wants us to flourish.

MALACHI 3:8-11 (NASB)
[8] "Will a man rob God? Yet you are robbing Me! But you say, 'How have we robbed You?' In tithes and offerings. [9] You are cursed with a curse, for you are robbing Me, the whole nation of you! [10] Bring the whole tithe into the storehouse, so that there may be food in My house, and test Me now in this," says the LORD of hosts, "if I will not open for you the windows of heaven and pour out for you a blessing until it overflows. [11] Then I will rebuke the devourer for you, so that it will not destroy the fruits of the ground; nor will your vine in the field cast its grapes," says the LORD of hosts.

8   Describe briefly your spiritual growth regarding giving.

9   What obstacles do you face in practicing generosity?

10   Often we have self-justifications for our disobedience: "I cannot forgive because . . ." or "I hate my parents because . . ." We will never convince God to justify our rebellion. Share a time you struggled but chose obedience. What was the outcome?

READ ALOUD
Tithes and offerings are expressions of worship to God. The principle begins in Genesis and continues through the pages of Scripture. We learn to be good stewards of all that God entrusts to us. Even our attitude toward giving matters. God encourages us to give cheerfully. The benefit of growing in generosity is the security of knowing God watches over our lives. Our well-being is not rooted in the economy or our financial statements; it is anchored by the faithfulness of God. We can live confidently, even in a frightening time.

11   How have you benefited from the generosity of others?

12   Think of someone you know who is consistently generous with his or her life and resources. What life lessons can you learn from that person?

Prayer

Close the session by reading this prayer together. Make it your prayer each day in the coming week.

Heavenly Father,
You have abundantly
blessed my life. Thank
You for Your great
provision for me.
You have provided
forgiveness, mercy,
righteousness,
justification, and
everything I need for life
and godliness. I rejoice
today in Your generosity
toward me. I offer myself
as a living sacrifice
as my expression
of worship. I will live
generously, cheerfully
offering to You my tithes
and offerings. I rest in
the shadow of Your
protection. You are my
Strong Tower. In Jesus'
name, amen.

PRAYER REQUEST

....
....
....
....
....
....
....
....

Daily Devotions

Day 1
God's Choice

³ *"Tell the whole community of Israel that on the tenth day of this month each man is to take a lamb for his family, one for each household . . . ⁵ The animals you choose must be year-old males without defect, and you may take them from the sheep or the goats."*

EXODUS 12:3,5

reflection question:

Is giving to God an arbitrary act? Why do you suppose He gave Israel instructions for sacrifice?

Day 2
Jesus an Offering

How much more, then, will the blood of Christ, who through the eternal Spirit offered himself unblemished to God, cleanse our consciences from acts that lead to death, so that we may serve the living God!

HEBREWS 9:14

reflection question:

As you meditate on the goodness of Jesus, ask Him to cleanse your conscience so that you may fully serve Him.

Day 3
Giving as Worship

"Bring the whole tithe into the storehouse, that there may be food in my house. Test me in this," says the LORD Almighty, "and see if I will not throw open the floodgates of heaven and pour out so much blessing that there will not be room enough to store it."

MALACHI 3:10

reflection question:

Do you practice giving as an act of worship? Try this month to intentionally give to the Lord and wait with expectation for His blessing.

Memory Verse

Proverbs 11:25 — *A generous man will prosper; he who refreshes others will himself be refreshed.*

Day 4
Be Generous

A generous man will prosper; he who refreshes others will himself be refreshed.

PROVERBS 11:25

Day 5
True Wealth

¹⁸ Command them to do good, to be rich in good deeds, and to be generous and willing to share.
¹⁹ In this way they will lay up treasure for themselves as a firm foundation for the coming age, so that they may take hold of the life that is truly life.

1 TIMOTHY 6:18-19

reflection question:

Think of a person you can encourage or bless today.

reflection question:

What are you doing to acquire true riches?

Study Notes

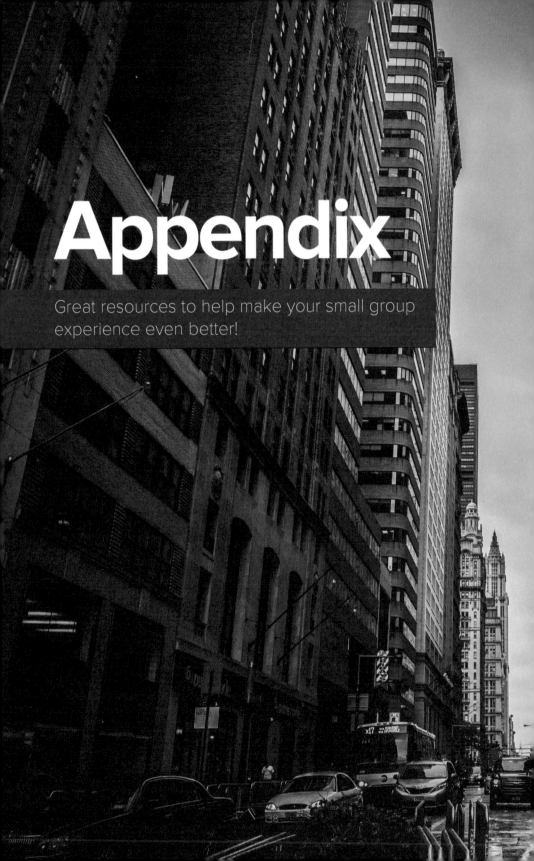

Appendix

Great resources to help make your small group experience even better!

FAQs

What do we do on the first night of our group?

Like all fun things in life—have a party! A "get to know you" coffee, dinner, or dessert is a great way to launch a new study. You may want to review the Group Agreement and share the names of a few friends you can invite to join you. But most important, have fun before your study time begins.

Where do we find new members for our group?

We encourage you to pray with your group and then brainstorm a list of people from work, church, your neighborhood, your children's school, family, or the gym.

No matter how you find participants, it's vital that you stay on the lookout for new people to join your group. All groups tend to go through healthy attrition—the result of moves, releasing new leaders, ministry opportunities. If you and your group stay open, you'll be amazed at the people God sends your way. The next person just might become a friend for life. You never know!

How long will this group meet?

It's totally up to the group—once you come to the end of this 6-week study. Most groups meet weekly for at least their first 6 weeks, but every other week can work as well.

At the end of this study, each group member may decide if he or she wants to continue on for another 6-week study. Some groups launch relationships for years to come, and others are stepping stones into another group experience. Either way, enjoy the journey.

What if this group is not working for us?

You're not alone! This could be the result of a personality conflict, life stage difference, geographical distance, level of spiritual maturity, or any number of things. Relax. Pray for God's direction, and at the end of this 6-week study, decide whether to continue with this group or find another. You don't buy the first car you look at or marry the first person you date, and the same goes with a group. Don't bail out before the 6 weeks are up—God might have something to teach you. Also, don't run from conflict or prejudge people before you have given them a chance. God is still working in you too!

How do we handle the childcare needs in our group?

We suggest that you empower the group to openly brainstorm solutions. You may try one option that works for a while and then adjust over time. Our favorite approach is for adults to meet in the living room or dining room and share the cost of a babysitter (or two) who can be with the kids in a different part of the house. In this way, parents don't have to be away from their children all evening when their children are too young to be left at home. A second option is to use one home for the kids and a second home (close by or a phone call away) for the adults. A third idea is to rotate the responsibility of providing a lesson or care for the children either in the same home or in another home nearby. This can be an incredible blessing for kids. Finally, the most common idea is to decide that you need to have a night to invest in your spiritual lives, individually or as a couple, and to make your own arrangements for childcare. No matter what decision the group makes, the best approach is to dialogue openly about both the problem and the solution.

Small Group Agreement

To provide a predictable environment where participants experience authentic community and spiritual growth.

Group Attendance	To give priority to the group meeting. We will call or email if we will be late or absent. (Completing the Group Calendar will minimize this issue.)
Safe Environment	To help create a safe place where people can be heard and feel loved. (Please, no quick answers, snap judgments, or simple fixes.)
Respect Differences	To be gentle and gracious to people with different spiritual maturity, personal opinions, temperaments, or "imperfections" in fellow group members. We are all works in progress.
Confidentiality	To keep anything that is shared strictly confidential and within the group, and to avoid sharing improper information about those outside the group.
Encouragement for Growth	To be not just takers but givers of life. We want to spiritually multiply our life by serving others with our God-given gifts.
Shared Ownership	To remember that every member is a minister and to ensure that each attender will share a small team role or responsibility over time (See the Team Roles).
Rotating Hosts & Homes	To encourage different people to host the group in their homes, and to rotate the responsibility of facilitating each meeting (See the Group Calendar).

Our Time Together

Refreshments:

Childcare:

When we will meet (day of week):

Where we will meet (place):

We will begin at (time): and end at:

Our primary worship service time will be:

Date of this agreement:

Date we will review this agreement again:

Who (other than the leader) will review this agreement at the end of this study:

Small Group Calendar

Planning and calendaring can help ensure the greatest participation at every meeting. At the end of each meeting, review this calendar. Be sure to include birthdays, socials, church events, holidays, and mission/ministry projects. Go to intendresources.com for an electronic copy of this form and more.

DATE	LESSON	HOST HOME	REFRESHMENTS	LEADER
Monday Jan 15	1	Bill	Joe	Bill

Memory Verses

session 1

Ephesians 2:10 — *For we are God's handiwork, created in Christ Jesus to do good works, which God prepared in advance for us to do.*

session 2

2 Peter 1:3 — *His divine power has given us everything we need for a godly life through our knowledge of him who called us by his own glory and goodness.*

session 3

Isaiah 40:8 — *"The grass withers and the flowers fall, but the word of our God endures forever."*

session 4

Ephesians 1:6 (KJV) — *To the praise of the glory of his grace, wherein he hath made us accepted in the beloved.*

session 5

Romans 8:32 — *He who did not spare his own Son, but gave him up for us all—how will he not also, along with him, graciously give us all things?*

session 6

Proverbs 11:25 — *A generous man will prosper; he who refreshes others will himself be refreshed.*

Prayer and Praise

Prayer

Week 1	
Week 2	
Week 3	
Week 4	
Week 5	
Week 6	

Praise

Small Group

leaders

Hosting an Open House

If you're starting a new group, try planning an "open house" before your first formal group meeting. Even if you have only two to four core members, it's a great way to break the ice and to consider prayerfully who else might be open to join you over the next few weeks. You can also use this kick-off meeting to hand out study guides, spend some time getting to know each other, discuss each person's expectations for the group, and briefly pray for each other.

A simple meal or good desserts always make a kick-off meeting more fun. After people introduce themselves and share how they ended up being at the meeting (you can play a game to see who has the wildest story!), have everyone respond to a few icebreaker questions: "What is your favorite family vacation?" or "What is one thing you love about your church/our community?" or "What are three things about your life growing up that most people here don't know?" Next, ask everyone to tell what he or she hopes to get out of the study. You might want to review the Small Group Agreement and talk about each person's expectations and priorities.

You can skip this kick-off meeting if your time is limited, but you'll experience a huge benefit if you take the time to connect with each other in this way.

Finally, set an empty chair (maybe two) in the center of your group and explain that it represents someone who would enjoy or benefit from this group but who isn't here yet. Ask people to pray about whom they could invite to join the group over the next few weeks. Hand out postcards and have everyone write an invitation or two. Don't worry about ending up with too many people; you can always have one discussion circle in the living room and another in the dining room after you watch the lesson. Each group could then report prayer requests and progress at the end of the session.

Leadership Training 101

Congratulations!

You have responded to the call to help shepherd Jesus' flock. There are few other tasks in the family of God that surpass the contribution you will be making. As you prepare to lead, whether it is one session or the entire series, here are a few thoughts to keep in mind. We encourage you to read these and review them with each new discussion leader before he or she leads.

1   Ask God for help. Pray right now for God to help you build a healthy leadership team. If you can enlist a co-leader to help you lead the group, you will find your experience to be much richer. This is your chance to involve as many people as you can in building a healthy group. All you have to do is call and ask people to help; you'll be surprised at the response.

2   Just be yourself. If you won't be you, who will? God wants you to use your unique gifts and temperament. Don't try to do things exactly like another leader; do them in a way that fits you! Just admit it when you don't have an answer, and apologize when you make a mistake. Your group will love you for it, and you'll sleep better at night!

3   Prepare for your meeting ahead of time. Review the session and the leader's notes, and write down your responses to each question. Pay special attention to exercises that ask group members to do something other than engage in discussion.

   These exercises will help your group live what the Bible teaches, not just talk about it. Be sure you understand how an exercise works, and bring any necessary supplies (such as paper and pens) to your meeting. If the exercise employs one of the items in the appendix, be sure to look over that item so you'll know how it works. Finally, review "Outline for Each Session" so you'll remember the purpose of each section in the study.

4   Pray for your group members by name. Before you begin your session, go around the room in your mind and pray for each member by name. You may want to review the prayer list at least once a week. Ask God to use your time together to touch the heart of every person uniquely. Expect God to lead you to whomever He wants you to encourage or challenge in a special way. If you listen, God will surely lead!

5   When you ask a question, be patient. Someone will eventually respond. Sometimes people need a moment or two of silence to think about the question; and if silence doesn't bother you, it won't bother anyone else. After someone responds, affirm the response with a simple "thanks" or "good job." Then ask, "How about somebody else?" or "Would someone who hasn't shared like to add anything?" Be sensitive to new people or reluctant members who aren't ready to say, pray, or do anything. If you give them a safe setting, they will blossom over time.

6   Provide transitions between questions. When guiding the discussion, always read aloud the transitional paragraphs and the questions. Ask the group if anyone would like to read the paragraph or Bible passage. Don't call on anyone, but ask for a volunteer, and then be patient until someone begins. Be sure to thank the person who reads aloud.

7   One final challenge (for new or first time leaders): Before your first opportunity to lead, look up each of the five passages listed below. Read each one as a devotional exercise to help equip yourself with a shepherd's heart. Trust us on this one. If you do this, you will be more than ready for your first meeting.

Matthew 9:36
1 Peter 5:2-4
Psalm 23
Ezekiel 34:11-16
1 Thessalonians 2:7-8, 11-12

PASTOR
ALLEN
JACKSON

From the humble beginnings in rural Tennessee, World Outreach Church has grown from 150 to over 10,000. Pastor G. Allen Jackson's vision is clear: "We want to help people respond to God's invitations for their life. We believe God is in the business of taking the ordinary and making it extraordinary."

The timeless message of God's redemptive story continues to be a focal point for the World Outreach Community. The congregation has spent the past few years reading and rereading through the Bible in a systematic way. The journey has been transformational, helping people develop a love and understanding of God's Word and giving them a memorable timeline to link the stories and characters. These 6-week small group study guides were developed by Pastor Jackson and designed for people to host small groups in their homes.

Pastor Jackson earned a Bachelor of Arts from Oral Roberts University, a Master of Arts in Religious Studies from Vanderbilt University, and studied at Hebrew University in Jerusalem. He has pursued additional studies at Gordon-Conwell Theological Seminary in Boston.

For more than ten years, Pastor Jackson has spearheaded regional men's events, drawing thousands. In recent years, these events expanded to include families and are held in Nashville, Tennessee's Bridgestone Arena.

Pastor Jackson is often a featured speaker at the International Christian Embassy-Jerusalem Feast of Tabernacles celebration in Israel. He is recognized by the Christian Coalition of the Israeli Knesset for his continued support.

Through Intend Ministries, Jackson coaches pastors across the nation and the world to greater effectiveness in their congregations. Pastor Jackson is married, and his wife, Kathy, is an active participant in ministry at World Outreach Church.

OTHER STUDIES FROM INTEND®

You've Got The Word!

X

EXTRAORDINARYGOD

THE FOUNDATION OF AN EXTRAORDINARY LIFE

G.ALLEN JACKSON
PASTOR, WORLD OUTREACH CHURCH

EXTRAORDINARY GOD
The Foundation of an Extraordinary Life

This six week DVD-driven study will take you on a micro tour of Israel with Pastor Allen. With each session, you will discover how our God demonstrates His great love for us through His chosen land, Israel.

Visit intendresources.com

OTHER STUDIES FROM INTEND®

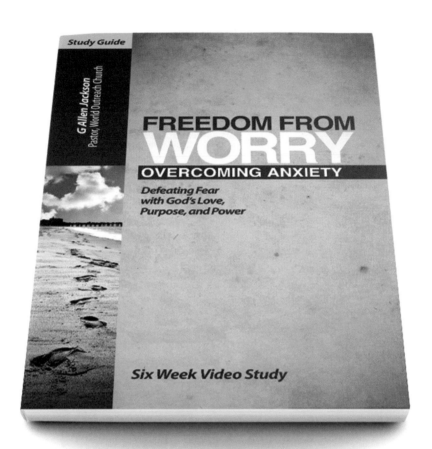

FREEDOM FROM WORRY

Defeating Fear with God's Love, Purpose, and Power

The Freedom From Worry Study Guide is designed to be used with the Freedom From Worry DVD and takes participants on a journey to discover life free of anxiety. Through these six sessions, Pastor G. Allen Jackson will teach your group to overcome anxiety with God's love, purpose and power.

Visit intendresources.com

OTHER STUDIES FROM INTEND®

THE WHITEBOARD BIBLE
A Three-Volume Study Series

The Bible tells a story. The amazing narrative begins with creation and concludes with Jesus triumphant. Between Genesis and Revelation is the story of God's interaction with the descendants of Adam. Through these sessions we will develop a twelve-point timeline, which will serve as the framework for all the characters and events in the Bible.

Visit theWhiteboardBible.com

For More

VISIT
INTENDMINISTRIES.ORG

*Providing tools and resources to help you intentionally
seek first the Kingdom of God*

Teachings from Pastor Allen Jackson
Weekly Devotionals
A Community Journey through the Bible
Mobile App, for our busy lives
Sermon DVD, CD and MP3

WEEKLY TEACHINGS FROM PASTOR ALLEN JACKSON INTENDMINISTRIES.ORG

THREE CROSSES SANCTUARY WORLD OUTREACH CHURCH